KU-595-902

AN INSPECTOR RECALLS

Selections from the Memoirs of Dr John Kerr

Retold by

JOHN G MUIR

Illustrated by
George J Glass

SCOTTISH CULTURAL PRESS

This selection first published 1995
© 1995 Scottish Cultural Press
edited text & biography © 1995 John G Muir
illustrations © 1995 George J Glass

Scottish Cultural Press
PO Box 106, Aberdeen AB9 8ZE
Tel: 01224 583777
Fax: 01224 575337

*All rights reserved. No part of this publication may be reproduced, stored in a retrieval
system, or transmitted in any form or by any means, electronic, mechanical,
photocopying, recording or otherwise without the prior permission of
Scottish Cultural Press*

British Library Cataloguing in Publication Data
A catalogue record for this book is available
from the British Library

FS\KER

896971

ISBN 1 898218 26 9

Kerr, John

An Inspector
recalls :
selections from
            F5 KER

896971

Printed & bound by Cromwell Press, Melksham, Wiltshire

CONTENTS

FOREWORD

My father-in-law picked up a copy of *Memories Grave and Gay* from a second hand bookstall some years ago. Aware of my interest in the history of education in Scotland he gave it to me to read.

I found this and other writings by Dr John Kerr, a schools inspector in Scotland in the late eighteen hundreds, to be informative, amusing and interestingly up-to-date in some of the ideas and recommendations he made with regard to education. I felt that many of his views and stories about people he met on his travels would fascinate and amuse people today if they could be retold and presented with illustrations and photographs.

In selecting and editing passages for inclusion in this book, I have tried to preserve the style and atmosphere of Dr Kerr's original work. I trust I have succeeded.

John G. Muir
Dornoch
February 1995

ACKNOWLEDGEMENTS

Memories Grave and Gay, and other books by Dr John Kerr, were first published by Thos. Nelson & Son, and I am grateful to them for their assistance in supplying me with additional information.

Thanks also go to: Professor Tom Bone, University of Strathclyde; The Scottish Council for Research in Education; Miller Academy Primary School; Sutherland Education Offices, Highland Region; Mrs K Allan, retired Headteacher, Scourie Primary School; Miss A Mackay, Aberdeen; and Mrs S Harper, Rothienorman: for supplying information, pictures and school records; Robert Toop, WEC International, for the picture of Canisbay Church; and Tom and Margaret Burt, proprietors of the Old School Restaurant, Inshegra, Kinlochbervie, for permission to use their line drawing of the school.

Dr John Kerr

In my quest for background information on the educational career of Dr John Kerr I came across a record of research done by Tom R Bone, formerly principal of Jordanhill College of Education, Glasgow, now Professor and Depute Principal of Strathclyde University. In his interesting thesis *School Inspection in Scotland 1840-1966* (Scottish Council for Research in Education, Univ. London Press, 1968), he makes occasional reference to Dr Kerr. Much of the following information has been gleaned from Professor Bone's work, and I am grateful for his kind permission to include it in this publication.

Dr John Kerr was born in Dalry, Ayrshire, on 15 July 1830. His mother died when he was barely two years old and he was brought up by his father who later re-married. He was educated at Dalry Parish School and, after being dux there, was invited, when he was only fifteen years old, to take charge of an adventure school in the town. He worked hard, attracting more than a hundred pupils to his class, and when he was eighteen decided to go to Glasgow University, though keeping on his school by employing substitute staff during the college terms. After four years in Glasgow, he went to Edinburgh University to finish his degree, giving up his school but tutoring private pupils to make money. He thought of becoming a minister, and attended lectures in Divinity Hall for two years, but eventually went on to Trinity College, Cambridge, insuring his life as security for a loan he needed. When he graduated there, and had coached for a term or two, he was offered the post of Assistant Classics Master in King Edward VI School, Bury St Edmunds, which he held for a year. In 1860, largely because of an 'especially hearty' testimonial from Rev. Montagu Butler, who later became Headmaster of Harrow and then Master of Trinity College, Kerr was appointed HMI in Scotland, one of only seven in the country at the time.

Thus, influence certainly played a part in his progress, but it was the influence of those who had recognised his merit, not of those who were friendly with his family, which was frequently the case in England at that time.

Not long after his return to Scotland, Kerr met Elizabeth Jackson, whom he married in 1866. They had five sons and four daughters.

Kerr's talents were widely respected and he had a long and successful career in the inspectorate as his record shows:

Inspector of Schools for the northern districts of Scotland, 1860-1878
Classical Examiner for degrees at Edinburgh University, 1867-1870
Classical Examiner for degrees at Glasgow University, 1872-1875
Chief Inspector in the South West District, 1878-1888
Senior Chief Inspector of Schools and Training Colleges, 1888-1896

John Kerr

In the course of thirty-seven years, he examined the majority of schools in Scotland, and gave evidence before almost all important committees. In addition to this he travelled widely in North America, Europe and Scandinavia and wrote in several journals about his experiences abroad. He published a number of works, including:

Cambridge Burney Prize Essay (1860)
Memories Grave and Gay (1902)
Other Memories Old and New (1904)
Leaves from an Inspector's Log Book (1913)
Scottish Education from the 12th century to 1913

As the extracts in the following chapters will show, his writings were interesting and frequently humorous. However, whether lecturing or writing he did not hesitate to criticise the education system of his day whenever he felt it prudent to do so. Kerr became an inspector at an important time in the history of Scottish education. In 1862, the introduction of the Revised Code (on the funding and supervision of schools) threatened to undermine certain aspects of education in Scotland. For example, it had been the tradition for the sons of gentry to attend the same schools as the sons of the poor. The Code defined the object of the grants to be 'to promote the education of children belonging to the class who support themselves by manual labour,' implying an enquiry into the social standing of the parents which would have been resented everywhere.

The Code also threatened the quality of Scottish education, when it was proposed that payment should be confined to the teaching of the 3 Rs, which went against the tradition of the parish schools to provide an all-round education which could take a clever boy to university. One part generally welcomed, however, was the widening of the examination system to include all pupils.

Later, alone among his colleagues, Kerr was to criticise the examination system also. His comment that the changes taking place as a result of the Code 'threw back our education for at least ten years' sound strangely up-to-date in today's climate of change in education:

At present all teachers may, and all inspectors must, work more or less in fetters... Percentage of pass, as being the most quotable test of efficiency, was by many the principal and by some the only aim. The clever child being sure to pass was allowed to mark time, while the dullard was mercilessly and injuriously drilled. The aim of many teachers was a low dead level for all... It is beyond question that the Revised Code demoralised many teachers by putting them on vicious educational lines.

That said, however, it should be noted that the average class size in the 1860s was eighty pupils – a challenge indeed by today's standards!

He was not slow to comment on teaching conditions, including buildings and resources for staff and pupils. For example, bearing in mind that slates survived for many years as tools for writing in Scottish schools, Kerr was among members of the inspectorate who complained early about their continued use in infant classes.

No noise more frequently disturbs the quiet of a classroom than the rattle of a falling slate, and when it falls on unprotected toes the results are serious.

The inspectorate were also concerned that in arithmetic, 'pupils still spent wearisome hours in the performance of elaborate calculations,' yet were often unaware of the principles underlying them. (*Plus ca change?*)

Whatever his superiors thought of his criticisms, Kerr survived to see the Code reviewed in 1872. By all accounts he was a popular inspector, and clearly an accomplished raconteur when dining in the manse or at the laird's house, where he would be welcomed during an inspection at the local school.

He was honoured with an honorary LLD from Aberdeen University in 1877. He was well liked in the North, it seems, and when he left there for Glasgow he was presented with a solid silver tankard, salver and breakfast dish, as well as a dining room clock. His wife received a gold bracelet and a silver tea service.

Professor Bone records that, in his speech of thanks, Kerr said that he 'refused to consider himself a machine, had endeavoured to make teachers feel that he trusted them and that they together had a common task in which they could help each other.' Such an attitude would explain why the teachers had liked him.

The Educational News of 21 November 1896 reported on a great complimentary dinner in Edinburgh arranged to mark the retirement of Dr Kerr, at which the chairman said he had acquired popularity everywhere without seeking it, and that wherever he went he was regarded 'an honest man, close buttoned to the chin, Scottish tweed without and a warm heart within.' When he rose to reply, the company stood and waved their handkerchiefs as they cheered him.

After he left the inspectorate, he continued to lecture and write and no doubt took time to pursue his favourite pastimes of travelling, curling, fishing and golfing.

Although he enjoyed fairly good health after his retiral, Dr John Kerr died quite suddenly at his home, 15 Royal Terrace, Edinburgh on 1 December 1916, aged eighty-six.

I

INTRODUCTION

Since my retirement from the public service five years ago, suggestions have been frequently made to me by a number of my friends about putting into shape reminiscences of my official life, extending over more than thirty-six years. To these suggestions I have till now turned a deaf ear, feeling that my experience presents few events of sufficiently outstanding interest to warrant my recording them.

This feeling is not materially changed, and I have grave doubts as to whether I am acting wisely in at length agreeing to do what my friends advise. They urge that my service has been the longest of all who have been inspectors of schools in Scotland; that I am the only one now alive who has had a share in the almost countless alterations and improvements in the work of the Education Department, from what may fairly be called its infancy, when only embryo codes had as yet existence, up to the present time; that, in addition to strictly official work, I have examined all the secondary schools in Scotland; that every county in Scotland has been more or less immediately under my charge, as either a district or chief inspector; that I have been classical examiner for degrees in Edinburgh and Glasgow universities, and have given evidence before all the important Education Commissions, the last being the recent one on Secondary Education in England. This is quite true, but I am far from feeling certain that it is sufficient to warrant my rushing into print at a time when, more than ever before, it is true that of the making of books there is no end.

It is possible that what I have to say may be of interest to some, and not unprofitable to others, but the consideration that has persuaded me to take up my pen is that I shall recall to memory many incidents which, in themselves, may appear commonplace, and almost colourless, but around which cluster many pleasant recollections.

I have occasion to refer to many old friends, but I shall endeavour to avoid such references as may give offence.

A man could scarcely have wandered over practically the whole of Scotland so long and so often as I have, without seeing some things and meeting some people with something noteworthy about them. I should be pleased to have the knack of presenting them in the their proper relations, with a correct sense of proportion and happy phrase. My observations will not be confined to matters scholastic, but may diverge on occasion into lines social, clerical and general. Illustration by means of anecdote may often be resorted to as the shortest, most graphic, and most memorable mode of exhibiting salient points of character. There is perhaps no scarcer commodity than a good new anecdote. To my intimate friends a large proportion of them will want the charm of novelty, but there are probably others outside of that circle to whom they will not seem so hoary and weather worn.

I do not propose to deal with technical topics that have been discussed ad nauseum in educational magazines, nor, except incidentally, to go outside of my own experience. I may have occasion now and then to make remarks on educational subjects that will appeal more to the teacher than the general reader, but such occasions will be comparatively few, both because I have not, so far as I know, any pet fads to exploit, and because it would be very foolish to make certain what, in spite of my efforts, is perhaps only too probable, that this little volume should be consigned to the limbo of unread or unreadable books. Educational deliverances are notoriously dull. My aim will be a plain, commonsense narrative of some things I have observed, approved, blamed, or laughed at during the last forty years.

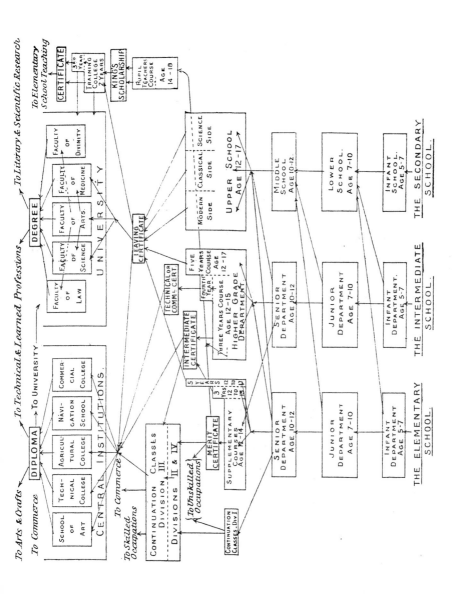

Organisation of Education in Scotland *c1900*
(The Annotated Scotch Code)

MEMORANDUM ON CONDITIONS OF APPOINTMENT OF INSPECTORS—JUNIOR INSPECTORS.

SCOTCH EDUCATION DEPARTMENT,
DOVER HOUSE, WHITEHALL, S.W.

1. No Candidate is eligible for the post of Junior Inspector whose age exceeds thirty-five.

2. Any gentleman who is desirous to have his name placed upon the List of Candidates should address a formal application to the Secretary of the Scotch Education Department, Dover House, Whitehall, S.W., to that effect, supported by copies of testimonials.

3. The application and testimonials should show the special qualifications of the Candidate for the duties of an Inspector of Schools, the University Degrees taken (stating especially the place and class of the degree taken in the final Schools), and other distinctions gained by him. As a rule, no Candidate will be appointed who has not received adequate training and had actual experience of the work of teaching in Schools in Scotland.

4. The Education (Scotland) Act of 1872 having established a system of undenominational inspection, no one who is in Holy Orders, or who is acting as Minister of any religious Denomination, is eligible for appointment.

5. The appointment falls to be made under Section 4 of the Superannuation Act of 1859. A Civil Service Examination and Certificate are, consequently, not necessary. A certificate as to the Candidate's physical fitness for the post will, however, be required.

6. A Junior Inspector will be on probation for two years, and his appointment may be cancelled at any time for unfitness or misconduct.

7. The Salary attached to the post is £200, rising by £15 a year to £400, and Junior Inspectors are eligible for promotion to the office of H.M. Inspector of Schools.

8. Junior Inspectors will be reimbursed the *actual expense* of travelling on the public service, and 1st class railway fare will be allowed. A personal allowance of £1 may be claimed for each night of enforced absence from home on duty.

9. Junior Inspectors must give their whole time to their official duties.

10. The ordinary annual holidays allowed to Junior Inspectors must not exceed thirty-six week days during each of their first ten years of service and forty-eight week days thereafter, exclusive in both cases of Christmas Day, Good Friday, and the day which is kept as His Majesty's Birthday, and (subject to the convenience of the public service) the four Bank Holidays.

11. The work of a Junior Inspector will be under the general supervision of a District or Chief Inspector, and his reports on the inspection of Schools and Classes will be sent to the Inspector for transmission to the Department. The duties of a Junior Inspector are subject to adjustment from time to time by regulation of the Department.

12. The Regulations as to the Superannuation of Junior Inspectors are as follows:—

A pension may be given at the rate of $\frac{1}{60}$th of *Salary* (at the time of retirement) for each year of service, up to a maximum of $\frac{40}{60}$ths.

No pension can be granted under ten years' service, nor claimed before 60 years of age, unless retirement is granted on the score of ill-health.

Superannuation Act, 1859, 22 Vict. c. 26.

13. Retirement is governed by Clause 10 of the Order in Council of the 15th August 1890.

EXTRACT FROM ORDER IN COUNCIL OF 15TH AUGUST 1890.

"10. It shall be competent for the Head of any Department to call upon any officer of such Department to retire at the age of 60 on such pension as by the length of his service he is qualified to receive.

"Retirement shall be compulsory for every officer on attaining 65 years of age. But in special cases the Commissioners of the Treasury may, at the instance of a Department, extend an officer's employment for a further period, in no case exceeding five years, on being satisfied that such officer's retirement at 65 would be detrimental to the interests of the Public Service."

Conditions of Appointment of Inspectors *c1900*
(The Annotated Scotch Code)

II

TIMES OF CHANGE AND CHALLENGE

A very rapid sketch of what immediately preceded, and led up through innumerable modifications and improvements, to the present attitude of Government towards education is perhaps not inappropriate to the purposes of these reminiscences.

About the end of the eighteenth and beginning of the nineteenth century there was a great educational awakening to the necessity of supplementing existing provision by Government assistance. Lord Brougham's Committee of Inquiry in 1818 revealed great deficiencies and destitution in the Highlands and Islands. This led to the establishment in 1824 of the Education Committee of the Church, which made great efforts to improve the situation, but with only partial success.

In 1833 the Government made its first grant in aid of Scottish Education in the form of a subsidy to the Training Schools and in 1839 a Committee of Council in Education was established. In 1861 the salaries of parochial teachers were increased, their appointment was transferred from the presbyteries to the university and any member of the Presbyterian Church could apply to teach.

The Education Act of 1872 was passed because the parochial schools were unable to cope with the demands of an increasing population. I feel that it is right to point out here what were the aims of the Government at that time in relation to the inspectorate. Inspectors were told that the inspection was intended to be a means of co-operation between the Government and the ministers or other managers of schools for the improvement and extension of education; not a means of control but of assistance; not for restraint but for encouragement of local efforts.

In 1860, when I joined the late Dr Middleton there were only seven inspectors in Scotland for all classes of schools except those in connection with the Episcopal and Roman Catholic Churches, which were under the charge of two inspectors for the whole country. Until 1872, all inspections were strictly denominational. There are now thirty inspectors and thirty sub-inspectors and they are kept as busy as the seven were forty years ago.

The number of inspectors did not then and does not now reflect so much the number of schools but of the schools taught by certificated teachers. Besides the parish and many other schools connected with the two churches, there were smaller ones supported by The Society for Propagating Christian Knowledge, the most of which were taught by uncertificated teachers. The changes here are very striking. Schools with a church connection have very largely disappeared; School Boards have taken their place and in almost every school the teachers are certificated. Every class is visited by the same inspector irrespective of denomination.

Dr Middleton's district included the whole of the north of Scotland between Dundee and Shetland, with the exception of Perthshire and the Western Isles. So thinly scattered were certificated teachers in these early days that the three of us managed more easily, but with a lot of travelling, to visit the schools than the present seventeen inspectors do today. However, we did have to stay away from home for months on end as we visited the many scattered communities throughout the north. We had many interesting meetings and adventures and I will try in this book to share a few of them with you.

We had time to visit, and did visit, many schools which were not in receipt of grants. Those interested in the success of any school had only to ask for an inspection and they got it, if other engagements made it possible. Many, many schools, badly ventilated, miserably furnished, and poorly taught have I visited in the north of Scotland, for which no grant was claimed or could be paid, simply to gather information regarding the state of education in particular districts.

These gratuitous visits were far from fruitless. While many of the teachers were old and hopelessly below certificate mark, there were not a few who took advice and, when the possibility of a certificate was suggested to them, set to work pluckily and gained the coveted parchment which they had thought to be out of their reach. I need scarcely add that they were all most grateful. In fact I never more fully realised that kind words cost little and are worth much.

[The following extracts come from the General Reports of 1865, 1867 & 1869 given by HM Inspector John Kerr Esq, on the schools inspected by him in the Counties of Banff, Moray, Nairn, Inverness, Ross, Cromarty, Sutherland, Caithness, Orkney, and Shetland]:

The majority of the schools in my district are small, rural, agricultural schools; a few are attended by the children of a fishing population, but the number of superior parish schools is considerably above the average of the rest of Scotland. This is due to the fact that two of the counties participate in the Dick bequest, a fund left for augmenting the salaries of parish teachers in the counties of Aberdeen, Banff, and Moray. One of the conditions of participating in this bequest is the passing of a severe examination, which almost necessarily requires university training, and those schools have, in consequence, been generally taught by graduates of Aberdeen or other Scottish universities.

In some of the more northern parts of my district, parents object to writing and arithmetic being taught to very young children, and refuse to supply them with the materials. I did not hesitate to recommend the teachers to refuse admission to all such, as probably the best cure for this.

Fees are seldom decently paid in the north. The parents are poor, but often more careless than poor; and habit is strong, especially where it lies in the direction of saving expense. They have not been accustomed to pay fees, and a change of habit is naturally not attractive. I have, in some of the more glaring cases, advised the rigid exaction of a small fee as the best means of making parents value the school, and as a corrective of carelessness at home and irregularity of attendance.

Irregularity of attendance is grievously complained of in many parts of my district, but especially in Ross, Sutherland and Caithness. There are many temptations to irregular attendance, but there is still more indifference about education on the part of parents. This natural indifference is unfortunately fostered by the very general non-payment of fees. Education costs nothing, and is consequently little valued. So great is the irregularity that if payment depended on individual examination, the teacher would in many cases earn very little, as only a very small portion of his school roll would be qualified by attendance. Feeling the necessity of some remedy for this, I wrote last autumn to the Duke of Sutherland, as having on his estates a very large number of tenants likely to be influenced by the expression of his Grace's wishes on the subject, and suggested that all the teachers on his estates should be requested to hand to his factors annually a list of all the children between the ages of 6 and 12 who, without satisfactory excuse, had failed to complete a certain number of attendances. Leaving a margin of 50 days for snowstorms, potato planting, &c., in addition to two months of vacation, I suggested that the attendance should be 300, i.e. 300 days, and that to all falling short of this his disapprobation should be intimated. I have received from his Grace and from his commissioners and factors, to whom also I submitted my proposal, intimation of their approval of the suggestion, and of their co-operation as far as possible. I shall probably make the same application to other large proprietors in my district, and I am not without hope that some good will result from it.

I have by no means been invariably satisfied that schools with the largest number of passes were on the whole doing most for education. There is a considerable margin within which a large number of passes may be obtained by means which, while not perfectly, may yet be so nearly, fair, and so approximately conformable to the letter of the Revised Code, that exception cannot well be taken to them. It may be represented that the children have a long way to come, and are therefore older before they enter; that the attendance is very irregular, and consequently less advancement possible, which may be wholly or partially true. And when none of these exceptional cases exist, the children may, according to the varying conscientiousness of teachers, be presented lower than they ought; so much lower as to secure passes for almost all, and yet not so low that an inspector would feel justified in saying 'this won't do.' Very high results under the Revised Code may be attained by an inferior teacher, for under it success implies vigorous *teaching*, but not necessarily *education*.

The number of passes is a comparatively valueless statistic, unless it is conjoined with the average attendance, the age of the pupils, and, not less important, the general intelligence of the school.

About the middle of April, schools in Inverness, Ross, Sutherland, Caithness, Orkney, and Shetland, begin to thin off; in agricultural districts, for field work; in sea-board districts for the collection of seaware for manure. In spite of my best efforts to arrange my visits most suitably for the schools, these counties can only be visited after April, when in many cases the attendance is little more than one-third of the maximum. In April last year I found in one school in Ross-shire only 37, while the attendance during winter had been upwards of 100. Again in October and November I have a few town schools which can be visited with advantage, but in the country schools many have not returned, and those who have cannot be expected, after an absence of five or six months, to do justice either to themselves or the teacher.

In a district so thinly populated as many parts of mine are there are many schools which, though small, cannot be discontinued unless the people are to grow up in ignorance. A considerable number of these, owing to their locality, and the possibilities of travelling, can be visited only in summer, which, thought the only convenient, and in some cases the only possible, time for the inspector, is the very worst time for the school, as the classes are broken up by field work, herding cattle, fishing, or by any of the numerous agencies in competing with which regular school attendance can urge but a weak claim among a poor population.

Where the parents are very poor, and a boy or girl of 10 years of age can earn as much in a day as will pay school fees for a month, regularity of attendance is, as might be expected, nearly at its minimum.

Since 1867 there has been a very considerable increase in the number of pupil–teachers. The uncertainty of tenure consequent on engagement from year to year which was at first a check seems to have become an encouragement to apprenticeship. The result is not satisfactory. I do not know many schools where pupil–teachers are appointed unnecessarily, but there are a considerable number in which their services are not commensurate with the expense. Pupil–teachers are, as a rule, of little benefit to a school during their first and second years. The present mode of engagement allows them to leave at the end of any year, and it is not all uncommon for them to do so just when they are beginning to be of use. Many who have no intention of becoming teachers are tempted by the stipend, and after a year, or it may be two, of very unprofitable service, during which they earn what is to a boy of 13 or 14 a large sum, break off and leave their places to be filled by recruits as raw and inefficient as themselves. The unsettled state of the education question in Scotland makes annual engagements inevitable, but it is for all that a misfortune.

While on the subject of pupil-teachers, I cannot avoid repeating what I have remarked in previous reports as to the insufficient professional training given to them. It is in my experience a rare thing to meet with one who is really efficient. Their influence as affecting the success, especially of a large school, seldom receives the attention it deserves. The fact implied in the name pupil-teacher is much too frequently lost sight of, the fact, viz., that he is a lad who is to be taught to teach. The cases are numerous where he is allowed to go on at his own sweet will, and to all appearance without ever having the advantage of a good, or the drawbacks of a bad, method pointed out to him. Wherever this is so the lad, unless he is a born teacher – and all boys are not so – is comparatively useless. I do not hesitate to make the broad statement that an inanimate, badly trained pupil-teacher is not only no benefit, but a positive injury to a school. He is simply a make-believe who is credited with doing work which he does not do, and which, if he were not there, the teacher would more or less successfully do for himself.

Scourie Primary School, Sutherland (1902-04)
Head Master: Mr Donald Macleod; Pupil teacher (**X**): Miss Mary Morrison

INSTRUCTIONS FOR KEEPING LOG BOOK.

Extracted from the New Scottish Education Code, May 1873.

rt. 34. "In every School receiving Annual Grants, the Managers must provide, out of the School Funds, besides Registers of Attendance,—

> *(a)* A Diary or Log Book.
>
> *(b)* A Portfolio to contain Official Letters, which should be numbered in the order of their receipt.

„ 35. "The Diary or Log Book must be stoutly bound, and contain not less than 500 ruled pages.

„ 36. "The Principal Teacher must make at least once a week in the Log Book an entry which will specify Ordinary Progress, and other facts concerning the School or its Teachers, such as the Dates of Withdrawals, Commencements of Duty, Cautions, Illness, &c., which may require to be referred to at a future time, or may otherwise deserve to be recorded.

„ 37. "No reflections or opinions of a general character are to be entered in the Log Book.

„ 38. "No Entry once made in the Log Book may be removed or altered otherwise than by a subsequent Entry.

„ 39. "The Summary of the Inspector's Report, and any remarks made upon it by the Department, when communicated by the Managers, must be copied *verbatim* into the Log Book, with the names and standing (*Certificated Teacher of the* —— *Class, or Pupil Teacher of the* —— *year, or Assistant Teacher*) of all Teachers to be continued on, or added to, or withdrawn from, the School Staff, according to the decision of the Department upon the Inspector's Report. The Correspondent of the Managers must sign this Entry, which settles the School Staff for the year.

„ 40. "The Inspector will call for the Log Book at every visit, and will report whether it appears to have been properly kept. He will specially refer to the Entry made pursuant to Article 39, and will require to see Entries accounting for any subsequent change in the School Staff. He will also note in the Log Book every Visit of Surprise (Art. 12), making an Entry of such particulars as require the attention of the Managers."

I welcome with satisfaction a growing tendency towards the substitution of female for male teachers in small rural schools. There are several instances in my district, and in every case the change has been followed by success. The teaching of the elementary subjects to a school of forty or fifty children is a task much more congenial to a woman than to a brawny able-bodied man. Male teachers in such circumstances often do little because they have so little to do. To the man who is ambitious to rise in his profession, the work is not sufficiently stimulative, and in the man who is not ambitious to rise a culpable acquiescence in the feeling that the duties are not quite up to the level of an educated man's work soon becomes apparent, and gradually degenerates into the perfunctory performance of doing less than the little required. With a female teacher it is different, she is more patient of the duties connected with the elementary subjects, and does not so soon give up working because the work is simple. Besides young children are more 'en rapport' with a female than with a male teacher, and the sympathy necessary to success is either ready to hand or more easily created.

Log-books are found in almost every aided school and kept, if not regularly, with at least an appearance of regularity. Every day has its entry, the value of which ranges from zero upwards. In some cases the entries are identical for weeks together, and I fear of little value, e.g.: *lessons given in the usual order; pupil teacher at his post in time*; after a month of which we find, as if there were some charm in the change: *pupil teacher at his post in time; lessons given in the usual order*. In other but rare cases the state of the weather as affecting attendance, the character satisfactory or otherwise of preparation of lessons, the removal of a class from one book to another, the commencement of a class in geography or grammar, are all carefully and judiciously noted. In almost all the summaries of annual reports are inserted, and thus form a continuous record of the condition of the school, valuable in all cases, especially valuable when a change of either inspector or teacher has taken place in the course of the year.

The log-book and registers ought to belong to the school as much as the desks or furniture. This is frequently not so. The teacher often purchases them, and on his removal to another school not unreasonably takes with him what he has bought and paid for. Some embarrassing cases have arisen when a new teacher on taking charge of a school had no record whatever of its past history, and was unable to fill up Form IX or the examination schedule.

What is wanted is the union of the education of the old with the practical training of the new order of teachers. Given this union, the valuable traditional custom of Scotch education would be preserved, the parochial schools would continue to be what they have been hitherto, though less so lately – the feeders of the university; the poor but clever boy would do what poor but clever boys by the score are at this moment doing at all our Scotch universities, viz., work his way at small expense from the condition of manual labour to respectability and position. The character of Scotch university life makes this not only a possibility but a fact. The constitution of the English universities makes it generally an impossibility.

III

The Englishing of Scottish Education

For those not involved in education, discussion on the Revised Code may be of little interest but I feel it is right in this book to highlight some of the weaknesses in the system before the Education Act of 1872, when a separate Scottish Department was instituted, and Scotland got for herself a code of greater elasticity and generally higher educational aims.

Prior to that, the Revised Code set Scottish Education back ten or twelve years and did great harm. In England, and in some parts of Scotland, educational reform was needed and to give credit to the Code it increased regularity of attendance. However, its plan was inherently mechanical and therefore bad in my opinion. England had little to be proud in its past elementary education that could serve as a solid superstructure, but even that little was completely ignored it seems.

Reading, writing and arithmetic for a considerable time stood severely alone. There was no suggestion about intelligence, composition, grammar, geography or history. The clever child was allowed to dawdle and mark time because he was sure to pass while the less able was drilled beyond his power of reception and to his injury. In other words, the highest grant was earned often in the most unintelligent and mechanical way, the intellectual life and tone of the school being wholly unmeasured by the inspectors.

This indictment is severe as far as England is concerned but is even more so regarding Scotland, whose past was the envy, not only of those south of the Border but of most other civilised nations. The old parish system provided, despite some of its failings, an education suitable for the dull and clever alike. That such a system was imposed on Scotland entirely as a result of an inquiry into the condition of elementary English schools, is a further indictment on the Code. Clearly it was assumed that there were no differences between our two systems and, more damningly, that Scotland was a mere appendage to England and did not require a separate hearing.

As most scholars know, in England national education was but of yesterday but in Scotland it was over two hundred years old! In Scotland it was not unknown for lads to go straight from the village school to the universities. As for teachers, in Scotland they were invariably graduates of good standing but this was not the case in England.

While some teachers managed to continue to maintain good standards the new regulations did mean that Scotland in my view stood still for ten years if indeed it did not go back.

One provision which proved to be the most obnoxious as it applied to Scotland was that children of parents in certain lower social positions could not earn for the school a share of the grant. This showed great ignorance of the equality of Scottish education for here the sons and daughters of the mechanic and the merchant, the labourer and the laird were taught in the same classes and sat at the same benches. The framers of the Code had clearly no experience of the healthy social mix in our schools and their view was clearly an English one, reflecting the social divisions south of the Border.

It is a fortunate circumstance that the Scottish Act of 1872 is as widely different from the English Act of 1870 as the respective countries are in educational tradition. In England it dealt professedly with elementary education whereas the purpose of the Scottish Act was to provide education 'for the whole people of Scotland.' The word 'elementary' is not found within the four corners of the Act. The decision by Mr Justice Wills in the Court of the Queen's Bench, that it is illegal in England to use the rates to pay for higher education, does not apply to Scotland. Such an action as that raised in Scotland would have no chance of success! The grand tradition of direct connection between the parish school and the university was not lost sight of.

Furthermore, from my personal knowledge as one of the examiners for degrees in Edinburgh and Glasgow, and from what I know of the pitch of the pass degree in Cambridge, I have no hesitation in saying what will be corroborated by all who have had the same means of judging, that the Scottish degree represents a higher level and a broader basis of education than the English pass degree. It is also quite certain that the preliminary examination for entrance is much more difficult in Scotland than in England.

IV

TALES FROM THE SADDLE

After I had visited the schools in my large area of responsibility once or twice using available railway, coach or hiring, I got the consent of the department to try horseback as a means of transport and several times rode from Dundee to John o' Groats and back. I was, perhaps, one of the last men in Scotland who did his travelling with a pair of saddlebags, with the bulk of my luggage going before me by rail or coach. I had a very complete equipment of waterproofs and suffered neither in health nor comfort from this (as some thought) risky mode of travelling over the north of Scotland.

I remember one noteworthy incident in connection with it. I had intimated the inspection of the school of Tongue in Sutherland and had to cross the Kyle in a ferryboat. My mare had a great objection to ferryboats and could be induced to enter them only by gentle persuasion and inch by inch.

On this occasion, she was unusually obstinate and completely exhausted the patience of myself and the boatman. At last, finding that the whole thing was taking too long, the boatman asked, 'Wull the peast have any objection to go into the water?'

'No,' I replied, 'she wades in quite readily.'

(By this time all the other passengers were getting quite impatient too.)

'Oh, that is goot.' Then, pointing to a tree about 100 yards up the Kyle, he said, 'You will be seeing that tree?'

'Yes,' I replied.

'And that other tree on the other side of the Kyle?'

'Yes.'

'Well, if you make her go in at the one tree and walk across to the other, she will not be wet above the knees, for the tide is out whatefer.'

I got into the saddle at once, and followed the boatman's instructions to the letter. All went well for a few yards, but the depth increasing, she lost her footing in mid channel and had to swim for about a dozen yards, before she reached terra firma.

I, too, found myself in the water, of course, and the first part of the inspection at Tongue School involved my drying myself in front of their welcoming fire.

I am inclined to think that Rorie, the boatman, had a more accurate knowledge of the depth of the channel than he led me to believe, but who could blame him, for his patience had been sorely tried. Neither I nor my good horse will quickly forget what I now recall as an amusing incident.

V

DRUDGERY OF THE YOUNG

O ne of the greatest changes I have seen in my years as an inspector has been the improvement in infant teaching. Until recently, the school life of an infant was drudgery, unrelieved by amusement or the healthy mixture of work and play.

The alphabet, and nothing but the alphabet, was their daily diet for a month or six weeks, or even longer under some teachers. When the lesson was over, they had to go to their seats and either sit quiet or make a disturbance, according to the teacher's idea of discipline.

There was no such thing as drill or other manual exercise to brighten up their miserable day. Even if it had been thought of, many of the teachers I know would have considered such things as silly and a sheer waste of valuable time.

Large town schools took the lead, but there are a few enlightened rural schools where the teachers, for fertility of resource in devising plans combining amusement and instruction, deserve the highest praise.

I visited England in 1884 and saw much superior infant teaching which, I am now pleased to say is evident in Scotland. In the management there was more repose of manner and gentleness on the part of the teacher and greater refinement and politeness on that of the pupil, than with us. Special training of infant teachers and less reluctance to send children to school before they reach the age of six or seven helped greatly.

In Scotland there was no encouragement for the development of new and superior methods. However, the prejudice against infant training has to a large extent broken down since the introduction, more or less fully, of kindergarten methods, and a Scottish infant school now need not fear comparison with its English rival.

There is, however, much division of opinion among parents as to the type of education they wish their children to receive. There is also much debate as to when they should start school. Educated parents are naturally among the most vociferous.

A well known lawyer was anxious to give me his views one day. He said that no child under six should receive formal education. 'The mind must be left to the free play of spontaneous observation of what is said and done around him.'

Sometime later, however, I learned that he had modified his opinion as a result of having a child of his own (a practical and not uncommon way of learning about children).

'We only began to teach him the alphabet when he was about six but, being so intelligent, he found it to be quite boring. I now feel that he was more ready to learn the alphabet when he was four and his intelligence less well developed.'

It seems that this change of tune occurred when struggling with a lesson at home along the familiar lines of 'A cat sat on a mat...' The child looked up in disgust at the stupidity of the language and said, 'Oh, damn the cat!' and threw the book in the corner. It would appear that the language he had learned at his father's table was not only more advanced but more forceful.

New and attractive reading books have taken the place of uninteresting, watered-down adult stories at the early stages, and the use of the Old and New Testament as reading books, with the attendant problems of language and meaning, has diminished. I do recall one or two good stories in a school in this connection.

'I'm in the New Testament now, sir,' one boy boasted. 'But I'm in the Bible,' piped up another in the room, as if to prove his superior attainment.

One teacher, concerned that the Bible would be less well read as a result of the new reading books being introduced, spoke to one boy in my presence who had discovered the interesting world of books. 'I hope, Robert, you read your Bible too?' he enquired anxiously.

'Oh, aye, sir,' he replied, thoughtfully, 'I do read my Bible; it has some fine interesting stories, ye ken, but man it has nae chance alongside *Wilson's Tales of the Borders*.'

VI

THE CLEVEREST LASS IN SUTHERLAND

Since the School Boards were established in place of the parish councils, I have noted, in some places, a marked decline in the interest of parents in what is going on in schools.

Perhaps it is something to do with the more strictly business-like but less sympathetic attitude of the Boards.

It was not uncommon for me, in former times, to arrive at a school to find that a number of parents were present as interested onlookers during the inspection. In connection with this I was told of an amusing conversation between two parents in the county of Sutherland on the afternoon of such an examination day.

Each had a twelve-year old daughter at the school at Kinlochbervie. Only Duncan, the father of one of the girls, was present. Norman, the father of the other one, was otherwise engaged.

They happened to meet each other near the little inn at Rhichonich, the vicinity of which suggested a dram, particularly as it was a raw day. The drams came and went and the two friends began in time to discuss domestic matters, including the education of their daughters.

'I think,' said Norman, 'the best thing poor men like you and me can do with our small savings is to give it to the education of our children; and we should give more to the lassies than to the lads.'

'Why should that be?' asked Duncan.

'Well, the lads can earn a fine living with a pick and a spade, but the lassies canna do that at all. If you give them a fine education they'll make a good marriage, though,' replied Norman.

'Faith, Norman, you're very right there and I'm sure that our Mary is the cleverest lass in all Sutherland. She's a grand scholar; I've seen to that.'

'Your Mary?' asked Norman, raising his eyebrows along with his glass.

'Yes, our Mary,' said Duncan, pausing only to sip his dram.

'Well,' Norman continued, 'I'll wager you that my Jessie is cleverer than your Mary.'

'And what will you wager then, Norman?'

'Another round of whisky, my friend,' was the reply with a twinkle in his eyes.

'Done,' said Duncan, draining his glass.

'But who will examine the lassies?' Norman continued.

'Well, I think I should do it, Norman, because, you see, I've just come from the school and the minister was there and the parents were there and the minister was asking them questions and the children would be answering them. I would be knowing well what sort of questions they would be asking.'

'Very well, Duncan, you go ahead.'

The girls meanwhile were amusing themselves outside. They were called inside, one at a time. When Jessie appeared, Duncan commenced.

'Jessie, your father tells me you're a grand scholar and as clever a lassie as Mary. Now tell me this. Do you know the meaning of a verb?'

'No, I do not,' answered the girl.

'That'll do for now then Jessie; just go away out and send in Mary.'

When Mary appeared her father said, 'Now, Mary, I have been telling Norman here that you're the best scholar in Sutherland. Do *you* know the meaning of a verb?'

'Yes,' in quite a triumphant tone, 'it's a noun!'

Duncan looked defiantly at Norman and said, 'There now, didn't I tell you she was the cleverest lass in Sutherland?'

'Well, I see she is certainly cleverer than our Jessie whatever and I've lost the wager, so we had better send for that whisky now,' he added contentedly, ringing the bell for the barman.

Inshegra School, Kinlochbervie
(now experiencing a new lease of life as a restaurant and guest house)

VII

THE SCHOOL WITH NO PUPILS

After the passing of the 1861 Education Act, which increased salaries and provided for the removal of incompetent teachers, a number of cases fell to my share. Even when the incompetence was unquestionable, I did try to act as kindly as possible towards them.

It was only on a rare occasion that dismissal without the usual retiring allowance was recommended. Most of the dismissals were sad but one I recall dealing with was highly amusing.

In a school in a remote part of Sutherland, the teacher, a respectable hale old man of over seventy years of age, as straight as a rush and as active as a ghillie, had been in charge for nearly forty years, and for about twenty of them had done practically no work. His pupils had simply left him; an arrangement which had his full acquiescence, as it left him free to indulge his taste for fishing.

The Duke of Sutherland's factor, anxious to avoid appearance of harshness, was willing to give him the whole of his old statutory salary as a pension and the continued occupancy of the schoolhouse, rent free. A generous offer, I considered, in the circumstances. Failing to get the old man's acceptance, however, he asked me to visit him to see if I could bring him to reason.

I made my way to the remote Sutherland community and called at the schoolhouse. He was at home that day. Taking me to the schoolroom, a receptacle for all sorts of lumber, the elderly headmaster did not react immediately to my gentle introduction to the subject. As we talked, I couldn't help noticing the solitary desk, which evidently had not been used for years, upon which lay all sorts of domestic articles and among them a couple of fishing rods and a basket. I pointed out to him that the terms were much more liberal than he could expect if an appeal should be made to the sheriff.

'But it is,' he replied, 'no fault of mine that I have no scholars. I am strong and well, and able and ready to teach them if they would come to me. Why should I resign?'

'I know,' I replied, 'that you are a capital fisherman, but as all the teaching in the parish for the past twenty years has been done in a well attended neighbouring school, while you have had no scholars, the sheriff would be quite sure to pronounce you incompetent, and in that case you would not get more than two thirds of your salary – and

no dwellinghouse!'

'But,' he insisted, 'I *have* had scholars within the last twenty years.'

'Have you really? How long has it been since you had scholars?'

He hesitated and raised his eyebrows: 'Well, it would be about twelve years or so.'

'How many had you twelve years ago?' (The conversation was becoming more and more amusing.)

'Oh, four, and sometimes three and two and the like of that, but it is not me that wud be driving them away. They wud just be going of their own wull, and it was not my fault whetever. I would be ready to teach them if they wud come to me.'

Clyne Public School - Sutherland
Summary of the Inspector's Report for 1884
(Dated 23. July 1884)

Though the Roll contains 124 names and the average attendance has risen by 21, the work is still carried on singlehanded. Despite this utterly indefensible state of matters the school fully maintains its position, thanks partly to the extraneous and unpaid assistance the Headmaster receives. The grammar of some of the senior Scholars was rather stiff, but with this exception the individual examinations, were, as a rule, passed most creditably, and the ready and intelligent answering in the Class Subjects was a special feature of the Inspection. The Children are very tidy and are very honest under examination. Singing is fair, and the Sewing classes are evidently carefully taught. Ink wells are much needed, also blinds. The Registers should be carefully checked by the Board at least once a quarter.

George Adams Correspondent

Clyne Public School, Sutherland
Summary of Inspector's Report for 1884

After much further talk, I felt that I was beginning to persuade him to yield and produced an agreement, which had been prepared in advance, for him to sign. I handed him the pen, which he accepted reluctantly, and I thought I had made my point. Suddenly, he became aware of this admission of guilt and threw down the pen angrily.

'Why should I resign when I am in good health and able and willing to teach? Will the Duke not give me £5 more as he did to my neighbour in the next parish?'

'No,' I replied, 'you cannot get more and you will certainly get less if it goes to the sheriff.'

He read the document once more, shook his head and, looking earnestly at me, said, 'Is it the good advice you'll be giving me?'

'Yes; I certainly advise you to sign it for your own sake.'

He took up his pen again and, shaking his head slowly, wrote his name, halting at each letter and indicative of a still possible refusal.

When his signature was finally completed and the ink dry on the page, I transferred the document to my pocket. I could not resist the temptation to confirm the real reason for the desertion of the pupils and said, 'Some people say that your fishing had a good deal to do with the falling away of the school.'

'Well,' he replied frankly, 'I would not like to deny altogether that it may have probably done some injury to the attendance.'

'You fished a good deal of course… just in the evenings?'

'Oh, yes,' he replied with a slight twinkle, 'and sometimes when I should have been teaching, I have to confess.'

'Not surely during school hours?' I exclaimed in mock reprimand.

'Yes, it's the God's truth I did.' Then, with increasing frankness. 'When the river was in good trim I would be givin' the boys a holiday or two. Indeed, you could say I did like fishin' better than teachin'.'

VIII

CLERICS AND CAITHNESS

There was a time when most teachers were either church ministers or divinity students. In my travels I met many of them who were not made very welcome by the communities particularly if they came from "The South", which in Caithness could apply as much to anyone from outside the county as an Englishman or a southern Scot.

However my first account springs from some trouble I had in a remote corner of Ross-shire. It was a small school and very elementary. The teacher was the local minister, a most unreasonable and ill-tempered man, who was continually quarrelling with his teachers. As a result, many of them only stayed a few months. I was sent to investigate.

Despite his calling, I found a man who was far from truthful and very far from being abstinent in the matter of strong liquor. His style of teaching was exceedingly confused and his results atrocious. I found the school in a wretched condition in almost every respect. The registers were very badly kept and none of the conditions, on which the payment of grants depends, had been met.

When I refused the grant, he wrote to the Department complaining that I had not examined the school properly, that I had passed over the Greek, Hebrew and many other things he said he was doing. There was, however, no Greek in the school and, as far as I know, we do not teach Hebrew in Scottish schools. The letter was passed on to me for my remarks and, on returning it to the Department, it was passed on to one of the examiners, a gentle conscientious fellow but one who is rather weak in analysing character. Added to this he had not much sense of humour.

After struggling for a long time with the confused English–Gaelic grammar of the teacher, the almost illegible writing and the reference to the overlooked Hebrew, he sent the document to the head of department, noting on it: 'It is very difficult to make out what this correspondence means.'

The learned gentleman, with characteristic quickness, wrote in reply: 'It is quite clear from his letter that this man is not quite right and, living as he does in the remote North, has probably a small still in the parish to which he readily goes.'

As a rule, the ministers, who had up till the 1872 Act been corre-
spondents for schools, welcomed the spread of Government inspection, and, wherever possible, chose for the traditional examination by
the Presbytery the day intimated by me for the annual inspection, and
shared with me the examination in religious knowledge. On one of
those occasions, the Rev Arklay of Inverkeillor told me of a previous
experience of his when the Presbytery were examining a school in a
fishing village. It is perhaps worth relating that there was normally
very sparing use of soap and water by the fisher folk. He was as usual
opening the school with prayer, when the door opened, and an urchin
with a face evidently fresh from the wash–tub appeared, and caused
one of the pupils to exclaim in the middle of the prayer, 'Lord Al-
michty, there's Jock White wi' his face washed!'

On another occasion, a clergyman who thought himself strong in metaphysics, but was thought by his friends weak in common-sense accompanied me to the examination of a school of very young children and opened in prayer, petitioning, 'Lord give these children adequate receptivity – that is, make them thoroughly to understand what they are taught.'

The relationship between minister and teacher was, as a rule, hearty and pleasant, and quite unlike that between the English elementary teacher and his clergyman. Oftener than not the teacher was one of the dinner party at the manse after the inspection was finished.

On the whole also, teachers were respected and well received by the community of the parish but there were exceptions.

I spent some considerable time in the most northerly mainland county of Caithness and, speaking to a former teacher from that area, learned that he had always felt a stranger in their midst. He was a native of Moray – a long way south, 'over the Ord' to Caithness folk – and he taught in the parish of Canisbay.

Canisbay Church
(Robert Toop, WEC International)

One day he was walking through the old churchyard there when he saw a number of tombstones bearing the simple but effective inscription: *Here lies an honest man.* His experience of the Caithness people, untrue I am sure, was very much to the contrary of this inscription and he penned the following amusing lines to make his point.

> *Behold how many honest men,*
> *Beneath our feet are found,*
> *While not a single one is seen,*
> *In all the county round.*
>
> *The reason of this circumstance,*
> *If after it you strive –*
> *They've buried all the honest men,*
> *And left the rogues alive!*

ADVERTISEMENT.

THE

MILLER INSTITUTION

Was Opened on the 1st day of April, and put under the direction of Two Teachers, both capable and respectable, determined to Teach effectively, at the following Rates per Quarter, viz. :—

For English Reading, Writing, and Arithmetic,	3s. 0d.
For all the above, with Grammar and Geography,	4s. 0d.
For all the above, with History, Writing, and Arithmetic to its full extent, including Book-keeping,	5s. 0s.

In the Rector's Class.

English Reading, with Composition, Latin, Greek, and Mathematics,	10s. 0d.
Or for Mathematics and French,	7s. 6d.
Navigation,	7s. 6d.

Thurso, April 1, 1862.

PRINTED AT THE NORTHERN ENSIGN OFFICE, WICK.

IX

THE GOOD OLD DAYS?

I noticed many great changes after 1872 when the Education Act of that year led to the end of the old parochial system which had been in existence for over two centuries in Scotland. The contrast, in respect of buildings and equipment, between them and the schools erected by the new School Boards is very striking.

The modern demands of this century of a certain number of square and cubic feet per child were, in many cases, neither thought of nor provided. The desks were often double, the pupils often facing each other, which in my opinion, was not very conducive to good discipline as they talked together and were generally restless.

The desks also were little more than flat tables, not sloping as they ought to be to contribute to good penmanship. Steel pens were not in general use and the making and mending of quill pens made a considerable drain on the teacher's time. There was often, even in large schools, only one teacher who, having many subjects to attend to, had recourse to various devices for saving time and securing efficiency.

A boy, well advanced in arithmetic, would sometimes be placed beside one at a lower stage, the former being instructed to give assistance to the latter. I have always believed that the best way to learn is to teach!

For the maintenance of discipline with such a large group, it was customary to employ a boy, chosen by the teacher and called a censor. He would stand on a high form, in a position commanding a view of the whole school, and call out the name of any pupil who was seen to be playing tricks on his neighbours, making a noise, or in any way breaking the rules.

The pupil so named was called out by the teacher and punished accordingly. I was not in favour of this method of discipline as it showed the teacher up in a bad light and led to ill-feeling against the poor boy chosen to tell on his fellow pupils. The 'clype', as he was known, was always unpopular and had a hard time in most schools unless, as was the case from time to time, there was a pupil who relished the power which was bestowed on him.

Although I have tended to feel that the parish schools could not cope with the large rise in the population, leading to more attention

being given to the bright pupils at the expense of the dull ones, I was intrigued to read recently of the remarks made by a French physicist who had the opportunity to compare the Scottish system of education over some time.

The Scots, poor and inhabiting a country by no means fertile, have risen by their education and civilisation to the level of a nation which is regarded as one of the most enlightened on the face of the earth. Wherever a Scotsman goes, the education he has received in the parish schools gives his mind a peculiar power of observation, and enables him to extend his view far beyond the range of objects which occupy the attention of persons of the same social status who have not been educated.

This, in my opinion, may be a rather over-friendly estimate of the worth of the old parochial system in the light of what I have said, but I suppose the theory of *a school in every parish* must be contrasted with the dearth of education in many parts of Europe at that time. Nevertheless, many of the changes brought in by the School Boards were certainly welcomed by me.

University of Aberdeen Local Examination Certificate 1893 - Alice Hay
(Miss A Mackay)

James Beattie, Shoemaker (1783-1867)
(Mrs S Harper, Rothienorman)

X

Lessons From a Shoemaker's Stool

E ducation in many parts of rural Scotland was sparse, to say the least, and the quality varied greatly. While in most cases an educated man, such as the parish minister, would be in charge and the quality depended on the amount of time spent on schooling, I met from time to time some most unusual teachers.

One of the most remarkable of these was an interesting old man, James Beattie, from the village of Gordonstone in the parish of Auchterless, Aberdeenshire. He was a shoemaker, but with his trade he also taught the children of the neighbourhood. For some sixty years he carried on what was undoubtedly a labour of love.

I had heard so much about him that I decided to call on this unofficial school on my next visit to the area. I knocked on the door one snowy morning and it was almost immediately opened by a stout man with well marked features but with eyes full of intelligence and kindliness.

'You are Mr Beattie, I suppose?'

'Yes, but come awa in oot o' the sna',' he replied.

'Perhaps when you know who I am, you will not ask me in,' I said.

'Weel, I dinna ken ony reason for keepin' ye oot,' he said, showing me in. I then explained who I was and that, while I had no right to demand to see his school, I had heard so much of the fine education in his place that I wanted to call on him.

'I've nae objections. Come awa' in oot o' the sna',' he insisted.

The schoolroom was a mixture of rough desks and items marking it out as a school, yet in the midst of other items which showed the trade of the kindly gentleman. Lasts, straps, hammers and old shoes lay among the shoemaker's stools occupied by only ten pupils. A number of empty seats indicated that many could not reach the place that day because of the snowstorm.

Almost as if I was not there, he carried on, still wearing his leather apron, 'Keep looking at your bookies and get on with your lessons and show oor visitor fit ye can dee.'

On setting them to work, he took over two stools and, pointing to the one near me, sat down to talk to me. 'You'll have heard of this

fine new school that is being set up nearby,' I said. 'Are you not afraid that you may lose some of your scholars?'

In the finest Doric, which I will not try to print, he explained that indeed he had heard of the place and that he was 'Thankfu' to Providence.'

'Why is that?' I asked.

'Weel, ah'm nae a young man, ye ken, and who will mind these peer craters when I'm awa?' he continued: 'They could all do wi' a richt school to attend.'

'That may be true, but you have done so well. Tell me, how on earth do you manage to teach and work at the same time?'

'Weel, ye see,' he replied, 'when they're doin' their ABC, I have to point to the letters and a canny work; but when they get the length o' readin', I ken fine by the sense if they are readin' richt and I can be listenin' and shoemendin' at the same time.'

All this he did most effectively as I soon found out. I listened to several children read and watched as he asked question, assisted his pupils and on occasion gently chided them for not doing their homework or not listening attentively. It was evident from the behaviour of the children that they all feared, respected and loved him.

I sat and talked with him on various subjects for a short time longer, and then rose to bid him goodbye.

'But, sir,' he remarked, 'this is a cauld day and, if ye're no a tee-toller, ye'll maybe no object to gang up to my house with me and taste something.'

I replied that I was not and that I would be very pleased to go to his house. We did so, I 'tasted something' and chatted further and looked at his extensive library.

I asked him if he took any fees for this excellent service to the community. 'Fees? How could I charge fees? But I must say they are all very kind and in 1835 they gied me a beautiful silver snuff box. That's it,' he said, taking it out of his pocket; 'Will you no tak anither pinch?'

I learned also that a year before my visit he had been given a portrait of himself and £86, some gathered from former pupils from foreign parts. He kept track of many of them and heard news from time to time of their progress in life. The most remarkable thing about this unique school is that there are now many fine scholars all over the world, in good occupations, some clergymen and teachers themselves, who owe their education to James Beattie of Auchterless, who taught them from his shoemaker's stool.

Thus ended my first morning with James Beattie in February 1864 and I felt as if I had been breathing an atmosphere as fresh, bracing and free from taint as that which plays on mid-ocean or on the top of Ben Nevis.

I saw him again in January 1865 and, though again a snowy day, there were twenty pupils present. The shoemaking and schoolwork went on as before; the awl and the hammer as busy as ever and his care of the bairns unabated. I saw the old man just once more. A few months after my notice of him appeared, his friends and admirers thought it their duty to recognise his noble work by presenting him with a purse of money. I was asked to make the presentation. I consented willingly and had the pleasure of putting into his hand a purse of eighty sovereigns. His reply was short and characteristic, ending with, 'I canna make a speech but ye ken I am gratefu'. It would be uncivil to refuse your kindness but I dinnae deserve it.'

I learned that he passed away in his eighty-fifth year.

Now Ready.

Price 1s. 6d.

Indispensable in Senior Girls' Classes and Evening Schools. In accordance with the Board of Education's Memorandum (Circular 758).

Lessons in Infant Management.

By FLORENCE LESSELS MATHER,

Certified Midwife; Associate of Royal Sanitary Institute; Author of " Hygiene and Temperance," " Home Nursing," etc.

T. NELSON & SONS, London, Edinburgh, Dublin, and New York.

XI

Laughter Defeats the Nerves

It is always an unnerving experience for a school and for a teacher to be given their first inspection. One of my first duties as an inspector is to put both pupils and teachers at ease if I am to achieve properly what I set out to do.

I was not long in my job, and still had some youth on my side, when I had to visit a female school in the little village of Auchterless in Aberdeenshire. The headmaster, a kindly man, but said to be of a hearty and impulsive nature, told me on entering the school that the teacher had never been inspected before and was exceedingly nervous. He asked me to bear this in mind, which I assured him I always did.

Not only was the teacher in a high state of nerves but this had been communicated to the pupils, who sat literally and proverbially on the edge of their seats from the moment I stepped into the room with the headmaster at my side. Seeing this, I made a funny remark, so much of an aside that I can't even remember what I said. It was enough, however, to produce a hearty laugh from both teacher and pupils more out of nervousness, I think, than in appreciation of my joke.

The final straw, which brought a huge response from the pupils and a surprised look from the teacher, was when he gave me the most re-sounding slap on the back with, 'Man, you're a fine fellow after all!'

The effect which an inspection has on a teacher was never put to me quite so clearly than by a young man whom I held in great respect. On each occasion when I visited his class, I commended him for the high standards which he maintained for he was indeed a great scholar and an excellent teacher.

Over the years, we established a relationship of mutual confidence and respect and I assumed that my visits no longer were held in dread by him. However, the true nature of our relationship was revealed when, after one inspection, which was as usual highly satisfactory, I bade him goodbye and, as I left, he remarked: 'Goodbye, Dr Kerr. There is no man whose face I am better pleased to see than yours, but I am always glad to see your back.'

XII

MORE HENS THAN PUPILS

For the first years of my official life, from 1860 to 1875, Orkney and Shetland formed part of the district under my charge. I have a most favourable opinion of the Orcadian and Shetland character. In it industry, self-reliance, and courage are combined with the gentleness more frequently found in women. In addition to other amiable qualities the people are exceedingly hospitable. Any person with a fair appearance of respectability can count on a most kindly reception at an Orkney or Shetland fireside.

My last visit to these attractive islands was in 1879. Since then, more frequent communication with an excellent service of steamers has no doubt wrought many changes and made these outlying islands much better known. But forty years ago, they were so little known that many persons, in other respects well-informed, thought of them as the refuse of creation, inhabited by a race with whom the civilised world had no communion; living on fish, dressing in sealskins; gloriously ignorant of cloth as we know it; destitute of any form of education, and, worst of all coming into this world and leaving it without benefit of the clergy.

Many thought they spoke Gaelic but, as is now well known, they are as ignorant of Gaelic as we are of Chinese. The islands were thought by many to have few habitations beyond Stone Age monuments when, as we all know, they have many fine houses and towns, not the least being Kirkwall, with its magnificent cathedral, more than seven hundred years old and a structure finer in many respects than that in Glasgow. It is in good repair, and a portion of it has been partitioned off and used as a parish church. This part has been thoroughly spoiled by pews, ugly square windows, and unsightly galleries, as ill-suited to the beautiful nave of the old cathedral as knickerbockers or a dress coat would be to a monk.

I had to visit North Ronaldsay, the most primitive, most curious and most remote of the whole group. It is also the most difficult to reach and I made four attempts to land without success. On the fifth attempt I succeeded.

I found eighty-one pupils on the school roll, and only eight different names. Every one is a cousin, uncle or aunt to everybody else on the island. The average attendance is thirty, but on the day of

my visit the weather was very boisterous and only five were present.

Shetland had only three or four schools in those days and I had to visit them each year. As there was only one steamer a week, I had to remain there for three or four days beyond the times of the inspections. I was given the task by the Department of visiting unregistered schools to induce more teachers to become certificated. In the course of this interesting but not always welcome task, I had some amusing encounters with them. They are known as missionary teachers, as they work both as teachers and lay preachers where no full time minister lives in a parish.

One such meeting was with a fellow who had not been long on the island and was supposed to combine the duties of preacher and teacher as best he could. I will not presume to judge his efficiency as a man of the cloth but it was evident that as a teacher he had done nothing!

I visited the schoolroom, which had obviously been long disused. I found it dismantled, part of the roof off, three tables that had served for desks, one bench whole and another broken. The sole occupant was a hen, perched comfortably on the joist, over which remained a fragment of the roof. The amount of hens' dirt on the floor indicated that more hens had inhabited it recently than pupils.

Not unsurprisingly, the teacher was not very keen for me to see the place at first and now I knew the reason why. Nor was he keen to talk about the work which he should have been doing with the pupils in his charge. On asking around the little community, I found many parents who expressed great anxiety about the situation and were keen to have proper schooling resumed.

I am pleased to say that there is now a fine little school there which is regularly inspected by my colleagues. I often do wonder whether or not the teacher still keeps hens and, if so, where?

XIII

MISSED BLESSINGS

I was informed by the Home Mission Board of the Church of Scotland that a deputation was visiting the remote Fair Isle. The Department encouraged me to take the opportunity to go to inspect the educational provision since a ship would be calling there specially and staying for a day.

We set sail on the cutter *Nelson* on a perfectly beautiful morning. After a very long sail we reached the isle, which lies between Orkney and Shetland. The cliffs appeared to me wall-like with no spot to land but the captain steered towards the east side where there were two little creeks suitable for landing.

A considerable number of people were visible on the skyline and they watched our movements with great interest. However, when it became clear that we were making for the landing place there was a simultaneous rush in all directions. I was very puzzled at this strange action. I learned later that the reason for this hasty departure was that they suspected we were the crew of a revenue cutter which called at the islands from time to time in search of smuggled goods from the Dutch fishing fleet which were then in the neighbourhood!

The news that ministers and not excisemen were about to invade them spread like wildfire and there was a great rush of men, women and children to greet us; as it was a day of fasting it was regarded as a providential occurrence for two ministers to arrive at the same time!

The missionary teacher was very keen to encourage the ministers to wait over Sunday to assist with communion but they pointed out that they had other islands to visit in the short time available. The other church members accepted this but the teacher was particularly insistent that we should stay over one night at least. When I quizzed him further when inspecting his school (which, by the way, was far from satisfactory) I learned that he wanted to make use of the presence of these men of God to get married as he was, in his words, 'Getting to the mature side of forty and may not have such a chance for a long time.'

The ministers suggested that it may be possible to hold three services throughout the island, thus fulfilling the requirement to proclaim the banns, even if all together in one week rather than over a period of three weeks as was the norm.

The fellow seemed to hesitate at this suggestion and tried to persuade us to stay overnight again. 'You see,' he said, blushing, 'I have not had the mind to ask her until just now. She may wish to marry me but, then again, she may wish to have time to think about it.'

I persuaded him to go and see his bride-to-be and he did. But he returned with a downcast look on his face. 'She says it is awfu' sudden and wants to wait until tomorrow.'

Unfortunately, the programme would not allow us to stay and we had to leave that evening. To the best of my knowledge, that lonely teacher on that lonely isle is still in the misery of single blessedness.

XIV

TRAVELLING TALES

E arly in my career as Inspector, I was stormbound for two or three days in Banffshire. Snow lay from three to four feet deep. The railway was completely blocked, and driving by any wheeled conveyance was impossible. I had most comfortable quarters in a hospitable manse, and enjoyed playing whist with the minister and his excellent wife and family, all well skilled in the game. The time passed most pleasantly, the only drawback being that my work was falling behind.

Believing that in the milder climate of Morayshire, (Elgin was then my headquarters), I should find it possible to overtake inspections already intimated, I hired two horses, one for myself and the other for a man who knew the country thoroughly and could guide me if necessary. We did eventually reach Elgin, but not without great difficulty. When I wrote to thank the good folks at the manse for their hospitality, I enclosed a doggerel parody on 'Exelsior', of which the refrain was 'To Morayshire'. It was an utterly worthless piece of writing, making humorous reference of a personal kind to my enforced idleness at the manse, and meant for their eyes only.

As it happened, I had rooms in the house of my good friend the proprietor of *The Elgin Courant*, to whom I read the parody. Unknown to me, he picked up the paper which I had left on the table and, in a copy of the *Courant* for that week printed it in full and attached my name to it. A copy was left in my room and, when I read it, I was horrified and indignant that my host had taken such an unpardonable liberty. I was certain that I would be the laughing stock of many of my friends and colleagues and went to the proprietor's room to express my anger. He was with two friends whom (I learned later), he had invited to witness my reaction to the article. Their presence did not prevent me from using vigorous language about what he had done.

After enjoying my rage for some time, he told me how and why he had done it, revealing that the parody was printed only on the single copy which he had left on my table! I had to admit that he had played a most successful and harmless hoax on me. Peace was restored and our friendship remained unscathed.

When I was not travelling on horseback or coach I made use of the many branch railways which had been constructed particularly throughout the North East of Scotland. In the 1860s, however, railway travel on some of these lines was primitive to say the least. I can recall a few amusing stories when I used to take the train to visit schools in that area.

One night, on the last train leaving Banff, I noted that the train was not in fact moving out at all, although it was well past the departure time. Having had a hard day and being anxious to return to my lodgings, I spoke to the guard about the matter.

'Weel, sur,' he commenced in the broadest Doric. 'You see I mun wait for Mr Fraser. He has a dinner perty the nicht and am gein' him twa or three meenutes preevilege.'

Whether or not the privileged gentleman actually arrived I do not know but we did eventually set off quite late, much to my annoyance.

On another occasion, when travelling on the Elgin-Rothes line I was surprised to see the Provost of Elgin running across the field towards the train which was going full speed. He had a letter in his hand; to my amazement, the train actually stopped and the guard took the letter from him, no doubt to ensure an early post! Can you imagine such a happening with the Royal Scot?

When visiting a little place called Ordens, no more than a siding on the Banff and Buckie branch line, I was informed that this was a request stop. As I assumed that one had to signal to the driver, and as I was returning at night, I asked how one should do this in the dark. I was told by the local teacher that the general practice was to set fire to a newspaper or other material which would light easily and would make a good blaze. On seeing this, I was assured, the train driver would stop.

As it turned out, the night in question was not only particularly dark but also very windy, as it can be on this coast. It was difficult enough to hold the newspaper, far less attempt to light it as I heard the train approaching out of the night. Despite my desperate attempts to get a blaze going, I failed miserably. In exasperation, as the train trundled passed the little halt, I gave an almighty shout, not really expecting to be heard and anticipating at that moment that I would be stranded in that deserted place until the next train came.

Whether the driver saw the flurry of newspaper in the darkness, or indeed heard my desperate cry, I will never know, but the train screeched to a halt just before the last carriage left the platform. I ran and jumped in at the end door in case he should change his mind.

Another little school I visited was near the track about a mile from the station on the Findhorn line. As the time came for me to leave and catch my train I proposed to leave for the station down the road, for fear that I would miss it.

To my surprise and amusement the teacher said, 'Don't take the trouble, the driver knows me well and always stops by the house in case I am wanting on.' And, sure enough, he did stop to allow me to clamber on over the shingle! Not surprisingly, however, I did learn recently that this line is now on the retired list.

XV

GOING BY THE BOOK

U p to 1872, religious, as well as secular instruction came under the supervision of the inspector. There was some concern among ministers of religion when this ceased on the passing of the Education Act of that year.

The gentlemen of the cloth insisted that 'use and wont in the teaching of religion will not be maintained and there will be the inevitable re-lapse into godlessness and heathendom.'

One teacher, in an excellent parish school in Aberdeenshire, held this view but I ventured to say to him that I thought his fears were groundless and continued by suggesting to him that he attached more importance to the character of religious knowledge than it deserved. In some schools I found that more attention was paid to Bible geography and history than such teaching as inculcates the practice of Christian principles and the moulding of Christian character.

Naturally he disagreed but I decided that I would test it to a certain extent in his own generally very good school which I was about to examine. When the highest class was brought in I commenced an examination of the Shorter Catechism. Effectual calling, justification, sanctification, repentance unto life, etc., were all repeated with scarcely a mistake by any pupil.

I then took up the Commandments, asking which one says that we must obey our father and mother? This was answered correctly. 'Which commandment says that we must not tell lies?' I continued. There was a pause and then one boy suggested the tenth, another the third and so on. With that, the dux of the class was smiling broadly and I thought that he surely knew the answer, but asked him not to speak until I asked the rest of the class. Failing to get an answer, I turned to him, 'Now then my lad?'

'There is no commandment uses these words,' he replied, smiling broadly. The minister was both surprised and shocked. However, I had made my point!

❦

In many parish schools it was not uncommon for my arrival to be greeted by an opening prayer in class asking the Lord to give me wisdom in deciding whether the school should continue to receive a grant or not.

On one occasion, when inspecting in one day two small schools under the same management, I was remembered in prayer at least four times. In the closing prayer at the end of the second inspection, the worthy teacher/clergyman prayed fervently that, 'I might have grace vouchsafed to me to give a good report of the schools.'

One is always reluctant not to be the means of answering a man's prayer but, as one of the schools was very far from satisfactory, grace did not abound to the extent prayed for!

Advertisements.

* In view of the enormous stress laid on the cleaning and disinfecting of schools by the memorandum of the Scotch Education Department, the special attention of teachers, School Board clerks, and managers is directed to this advertisement. Jeyes' Sanitary Compounds have stood the test of actual experience in a large number of schools, and have won golden opinions from education authorities and medical men. "CYLLIN" is now a household word in the schools.   Editor, "Annotated Scotch Code."

By Royal Warrants

To H.M.   To H.M.
King George V.   Queen Alexandra.

Disinfection of Schools*

AVOID SCHOOL EPIDEMICS AND COMPLAINTS
(Measles, Scarlet Fever, Ringworm, Etc.)

By Using Daily

JEYES' DISINFECTANTS.

JEYES' FLUID, for Lavatories, Etc.

JEYES' SPECIAL FLUID CYLLIN, for Watering Floors and Spraying Walls, Corridors, Cloak Rooms, Etc.

JEYES' CYLLIN LIQUID SOAP, for Washing Floors, Desks, Seats, Etc.

JEYES' CYLLIN SOAP, for Children's Hands.

JEYES' CYLLIN SOFT SOAP, for Children's Heads.

JEYES' SWEEPING POWDER, in Casks.

Particulars of the most efficient method of disinfecting schools can be obtained free on application to—

JEYES' SANITARY COMPOUNDS CO., Ltd.,
64 CANNON STREET, LONDON, E.C.

44

H.M. Inspector's Report date 22nd June 1867.

"Both under individual examination and generally, the School made a good appearance. Grammar and Geography are well taught.

Examination would be much facilitated by the children being trained to speak in a louder voice"

H.M. Inspector's Report dated 30th June 189.

"This School is conducted with great earnestness and activity and the standards passed very well, of 14 presented none failing except 4 in Arithmetic. Other subjects are well taught; Grammar more fully than usual; Geography good and full; Religious Knowledge very good. The use of the fingers should be discontinued and a ball frame provided. The discipline might be more thorough, and the children should be made to speak with greater distinctness."

John Kerr H M I

Extract from HM Inspector's Report, Rogart School, Sutherland

XVI

APPEARANCE COUNTS

I learned that the manner and neatness of my dress was at all times noticed as the following incidents will convey. It appears that on more than one occasion I was not as fastidious as necessary as to necktie, buttonhole and general "get up" some think a man of my status should be.

On one occasion, when my knowledge of Aberdeenshire was very imperfect, the minister of Rhynie, whose parish school I was to visit, wrote to me to say that I should travel by rail to Gartly, and that his servant would meet me with a gig.

I took his advice and arrived at the station comfortably dressed in a winter costume, roughish greatcoat and wide-awake hat. I saw a gig at the station, the driver of which was evidently on the outlook for some one. He looked at me, but it was quite clear that I did not come up to his expectation of the person he was sent to meet. I fancy he expected to see a person faultlessly dressed, and with at any rate the finishing touches of tall hat. While he kept looking round for such a person, and quite overlooking me, I went up to him and asked if he came from the manse of Rhynie.

'Yes,' he replied, in a tone in which combined respect and disappointment were quite evident, and with a glance at my hat, 'Are ye the Government?' I said I was and got into the gig, feeling, however, that I had seriously lowered his respect for a Government official.

Another experience a few days later led me to suspect that my dress was indeed not what it should have been. My work for a fortnight or so was in the neighbourhood of Huntly, which I intended to make my headquarters for the time. I had a considerable amount of writing to do and, wishing to avoid the bustle and noise of a hotel, I decided to take private lodgings. Suitable quarters were recommended to me, with two comfortable rooms in a quiet part of town. I said to the landlady that they would suit me very well and asked if I could have them.

'How long will you be wanting them for?' she asked.

'A fortnight or so,' I replied.

'Ah! I never let my rooms for less than a month.'

'I am very sorry they would suit me nicely but I cannot possibly stay for a month,' and made a step towards the door.

Clearly not wishing the rooms to be unlet, the lady turned an inquisitive eye on me, and said, 'Will you be much in the house when you are here?'

Amused at the question and beginning to fence, I replied, 'I shall be both in and out a great deal.'

'Will you be out at night?'

'Not much, and at any rate, not very late.'

Failing to make much headway by these questions, she went direct to the point. 'What will you be doing when you are here?'

I told her then my business in Huntly and she then said with many apologies, 'Oh, you'll have the rooms for as long or as short as you like; it's just that some folks were coming to give concerts here and I thought you looked as if you may be one of them!'

XVII

SOME LAUGHS FROM THE TRAINING COLLEGE

F or a number of years I spent a week or two in Glasgow in connection with Training College examinations. The somewhat dreary work of revising papers of candidates for admission to the colleges and for teachers' certificates was occasionally relieved by deliciously ludicrous answers. I have notes of many of them, a few of them bear being recorded.

Twenty years ago the examination papers had the questions printed on the margin with ample space opposite for the written answers. A paper on school management proved a very hard nut to crack for Norman, a poor lad from the Western Isles. One question was:

Draw up a specimen of a time-table for a school of 120 scholars conducted by one teacher and two pupil-teachers.
To do this properly, having regard to the different branches to be taught, the time due to each, and the proper employment of the three members of staff during four or five school hours, twenty minutes or half an hour would not be an unreasonable allowance. Poor Norman's duty was to quote the number of the question, and write the answer on the ample space opposite. A time-table was something entirely new to him, and he felt he had not much to say. He thought, however, that he might as well fill up the space appointed, and accordingly wrote out, quite unnecessarily, in a good bold hand, the heading of the question – 'Specimen of a time-table...' etc. – and below it the answer: *A while at every class* – and not a word more! The next question was:

Explain what is meant by education, instruction and teaching as distinguished from each other. This was dealt with in the same way, and the answer, short and comprehensive, was: *Education is to give us the knowledge of everything in this world and the world to come.* The third question which he attempted to answer was:

Give four or five practical rules for the guidance of a teacher with reference to punishment – and the answer: *First lash him, then take off his trousers, then make him stand on a stool in the presence of the scholars, then put him out of the school.* (I wonder if he was speaking from experience!)

Another Highland lad, in answer to the question of punishment, wrote: *When the child would come late to school, I make him to go the bottom of the class, and to allow all the class to moke [sic] him and to explain to him that he was doing a great loss to himself. I would expect that this would cure him a little in coming earlier.*

In a paper on domestic economy, one of the questions suggested a comparison between the duck and the hen. One girl, while describing the duck most accurately otherwise finished with: *It has an awkward waddling gait, because its hindlegs are longer than its fore ones.* Thinking this to be an unconscious slip I read on only to find her description of the hen ending with the remark: *The hen has not an awkward, waddling gait, because it has only two legs.* On the same paper there was a question:

Give reasons for avoiding extreme neatness and extreme slovenliness in dress. After a few very sensible remarks she wound up with: *It is a great sin to waste much time or money upon dress. Our first parents were naked and were not ashamed.* She was, doubtless, quite unconscious of the logical consequence of her answer.

Another girl, in giving a recipe for the making of Scottish broth got on beautifully until she wrote: *A few leeches may now be added if onions can't be had.*

In dealing with answers to examination papers the examiner is much more apt to note absurdities for their piquancy, than to record the unobtrusive merit of sound attainment. A good full-blooded blunder has a distinct conversational value in being usually short and quotable, and always amusing. The produce of a healthy brain and hard work has none of these qualities, and is passed over unrecorded. While I have highlighted blunders and still have others worth recording, it would be grossly unfair to represent them as typical of the education given in training colleges, or a measure of the mental calibre of students generally.

XVIII

CONCERNING CORPORAL PUNISHMENT

T he question of corporal punishment in the maintenance of discipline is by no means a simple one. I have only once or twice seen the tawse used during the annual inspection, but at visits without notice, in passing from room to room, I have both seen and heard it vigorously administered by both sexes in the staff of juvenile departments. On every occasion when it was seen that I observed it, the instrument was immediately huddled out of sight, as if the teacher had a feeling that everything was not quite right. That it can be entirely dispensed with is, I think, impossible; that it is much more common than it ought to be, and is resorted to as being the most expeditious, and, to the teacher, the least troublesome exercise of discipline is, I am satisfied, quite certain.

It is often due not so much to the pupil being naughty as to the teacher being injudicious. It should not be much needed in roomy, well-ventilated schools, where the pupils are physically comfortable. It should be used only for moral offences, such as falsehood, cheating and disobedience, and then only when other means have been tried and failed. It is beyond doubt that the teacher who punishes the least is the best disciplinarian. In no school where the teacher takes the trouble to make careful observation of character, moral or mental, ought corporal punishment to be anything but a matter of rare occurrence. Sympathy with inferior mental power in one class of pupil, and with nervousness in another, would enormously diminish the number of cases in which physical pain is regarded as a corrective. It is simply cruel and permanently injurious to punish for shortcomings resulting from dullness or nervousness.

A very noteworthy example of excellent discipline is told of a famous Aberdeen teacher, Dr Melvin. He is said to have scarcely ever had recourse to corporal punishment. On one very serious occasion he was compelled to depart from his almost invariable rule.

He called up the offender and said, 'James I am going to punish you, and you must be a very bad boy, and have done something very wrong, for I have not punished a boy for seven years. But I must punish you today, and very sorry I am.' After a few more remarks, firm but kindly, about the nature of the offence, he took his keys from his pocket, opened the desk, and took out the tawse that had been lying with dust of seven years upon it, and said, 'James, hold out your hand.'

James did so, and the teacher, grasping the instrument of torture in his right hand, and raising it aloft, brought it down very, very slowly and, with the lightness of a feather, touched the lad's palm. 'Now, James, go to your seat.'

James went, laid his head on the desk and cried as if his heart would break. He had not been hardened by the daily contemplation of flogging, and he felt that there was contamination in the very touch of the tawse. Perhaps none but a strong man could rise to this height of discipline, but weaker men might take it as an example, and probably the strength would come.

PRICE LIST.

School Straps, light weight,   9/6 each
    Do.   medium   „   10/-   „
    Do.   heavy   „   10/6   „
    Do. extra heavy   „   11/-   „

INCLUSIVE OF POSTAGE.

JOHN J. DICK,
(Successor to R. PHILP & SON),

150 MAIN STREET,   **LOCHGELLY, FIFE.**

XIX

IMPROVING TEACHER TRAINING

I had under my charge, during the first sixteen years of my service, the counties of Aberdeen, Banff and Moray, in which, the parish schools were almost invariably filled by men who had a full university course. In view of prospective legislation which might interfere with the continuance of this, and of the fact that, in a number of cases elsewhere in Scotland, men of purely Normal School training had been appointed to parish schools, it seemed probable that in the course of a few years the majority of our schools would be similarly staffed. I therefore thought it important to consider how far the curriculum of the Normal School was fitted to furnish a body of teachers who could maintain the fine tradition of the old parish school.

There can be no doubt that it was totally unfit. The various training colleges did their work faithfully and well, but they did not cover more than the fringe of higher subjects, for the good reason that the average pupil-teacher was not prepared to receive more.

In my first general report for 1865 I pointed this out, and sketched roughly a scheme by which attendance at the university might be con-joined with the Normal College Training without injury to the latter. During the two years that followed before a second general report was required of me, I had a very large amount of communication, personal and written, with Sir Francis Sandford, and the rectors of the four training colleges then existing, as to its feasibility. The result was general approval.

There followed considerable changes in the curriculum of the train-ing colleges; but they were carried out gradually, and have been di-rected in almost every case towards something more robust and educative than the prescriptions of the early syllabus. For example, I found that the most distasteful and harassing task of the students was the committing to memory for repetition, and repetition only, of three hundred lines of poetry in both the first and second years of training. This seemed to me more of a school than a college exercise and made a drain on the student's time out of all proportion to its usefulness. I obtained the consent of the Department to its abolition.

I observed that instruction in French and German was entirely confined to translation and grammatical drill; that attention to pronunciation was in most of the colleges nil and in none sufficient, because it was not tested, and carried no marks in examination. Further, the majority of students left the colleges nominally qualified to teach a language, their pronunciation of which was absolutely unrecognisable.

I also wished to see the substitution of experimental laboratory work for mere bookwork in science. In all of the science subjects the course is now one of first-hand investigation of the actual facts of the science, with as little reference as possible to text books. Lord Balfour as Chancellor of St Andrew's University stressed that a modern university must deal with principles and encourage original research. There is no better way to achieve this than by training our teachers in personal investigation of the science subjects they are to teach. School education conducted on these lines, and with steady regard to underlying principles, cannot fail to influence university teaching, and so make school and university act and react on each other. This is doubtless the motive of the change.

In England all training colleges are residential but in Scotland only two of them are. For students not in residence there is a tendency for them to overwork and not eat sufficient food. It has been found that strain can overtake students who do not have a substantial midday meal. By an appeal to those interested in education I set on foot in 1893 a movement in Edinburgh for providing, for such students as chose, a plain nourishing dinner at a price within their moderate means. The scheme has been beyond expectation successful.

XX

HIGHLAND CUSTOMS

E very man who has travelled much in the Highlands must have observed that, when he has reached a certain degree of latitude, the morning dram is a preliminary to breakfast in practically every house in which the *menage* is fairly comfortable, or in what may be called a "bien house" whether it be the house of a minister, a well-to-do farmer or a laird. This at any rate was the case thirty years ago. It is usually called 'bitters' and it often is a mixture of bitters and whisky.

It would be natural to infer from this that the Highlander must be more drunken than the Lowlander. So far as I have observed, such an inference is unwarranted. It is usually a very small drop, about one fourth of a wine glass or less. When I visited Russia in 1897 I found the same custom prevalent on board Swedish and Russian steamers and in restaurants, and Swedes and Russians of that social class are not a notoriously intemperate people. I am unable to account for the custom and I am not concerned to maintain that it is a good one!

It may be due to climatic conditions common to Sweden, Russia and the Highlands and Islands of Scotland. If I am to believe the account given to me by a hotelkeeper in the west of Ross-shire, I should consider the climate as indeed the cause, as Englishmen, when exposed to the same conditions, take kindly to the custom.

Some thirty years ago I was staying in the Balmacara Hotel, near Strome Ferry. During my stay there a sale was to take place at a large farm in the neighbourhood. The ferry crossings at Kylerhea and Kyleakin are sometimes very troublesome, and farmers from considerable distances had come to the hotel on the night before the sale in view of possibly bad weather.

On going into the dining room for breakfast, I found it full of these visitors and the landlord, Mr Macrae, going round with the 'bitters'. When in due course he came to me I asked in joke if it were not a bad thing to drink whisky before breakfast.

'Oh no,' he replied, 'it is a very good old custom.'

'But,' I said, 'if English people saw us taking whisky in the morning they would think we were a very drunken lot.'

'Well,' he replied, 'I'll tell you my experience. When the Englishmen will come here, I'll give them a drop like the rest, and they'll pull a very ugly face and say, "Ach, Macrae, it's very bad this!" I'll never mind them, but I persevere for three or more days and give them a small drop every morning. And, do you know, they find it does them good, and they come to like it. They then call it a "tonic", take it every morning whatever, and pull ugly faces no more.'

Mr Macrae's illustration is corroborated by the experience of an Englishman on his first visit to Scotland. He was an oldish gentleman, but very plucky, and made good use of his visit, even at the cost of personal inconvenience. He paid a visit to the island of Arran where a company of volunteers were camping out. They were to change guard at an early hour in the morning, and the old gentleman, having resolved to do everything thoroughly, made for the camping ground. It was a cold raw morning and his nose was blue and moist. He looked the picture of discomfort and couldn't help railing against the climate and the weather as being the worst he had ever experienced.

A friend of mine near him took pity on him and gave him from his flask a glass of undiluted whisky. It had not reached its destination more than a few minutes when he turned round, rubbing his hands gleefully and with a beaming countenance exclaimed, 'Well 'pon my word, this is a glorious morning.'

I am assured that the custom has now to a large extent died out. I wonder if the Highland climate is more temperate nowadays?

XXI

TRADITION AND SUPERSTITION

There are several other respects in which, especially in the Highlands, great changes have taken place during the latter part of the nineteenth century. Thanks to railways and greater contact with the South, the exceedingly narrow views of former times in respect of Sabbath Observance have given place to what is broader, healthier and more rational. In few districts now would shaving on Sunday be thought Sabbath desecration. But not more than thirty years ago a minister told me that in performing that simple and necessary operation he found it imperative to shut his dressing-room door most carefully, lest his servants should see him shaving, raising a scandal in the parish, and he be regarded as sitting in the chair of the scorner.

A Sutherland crofter who, on his deathbed, while bewailing his shortcomings, confessed to having stolen a sheep two years previously; a theft which had not been proved against anyone. The minister to whom he made the confession hoped he had prayed for forgiveness.

'Yes,' said the man; 'but that's not the biggest sin I have committed.'

'What else have you done?' asked the minister.

'Well, sir,' he replied, 'there was a Sabbath I did not go to church for I was not well and I was very thirsty, for it was a warm day, and I went out to the well and brought in a canful of water, and I cannot get the sin out of my head.'

Either the man wished to have the favour of his minister in such a confession or he genuinely felt guilt at his actions. Under either supposition, morality fares badly.

I have heard of a more humorous side to such accounts of Sabbath Observance, however. Fishing is a favourite pastime with the schoolmaster, although I hear that golf is taking its place with some. Not, however for a man I knew in the North. He was so fond of fishing that he even set his lines on a Saturday night and found a quiet hour the next day when he went to see the success of his Sabbath breaking. He was found out and was severely reprimanded by the kirk session.

This did not check his passion, however, and a friend thought to teach him a lesson. Under cover one night he removed the bait from the line and replaced it with a red herring in the hope that a smoked fish would indicate to Donald the hot quarter from which it had come and which if he went on sinning would be his own ultimate destination.

The next day, Donald took the red herring off the hook, smelt it and was overheard saying, 'This fush was smoked with sawdust or seaweed, and I never heard of anything but brimstane being burned down yonder. Ye are not so clever, Murdo Mackay.'

At this time the Lord's Supper was regarded in the Highlands not as a means of grace but as a test of discipleship, and it was accordingly thought almost sacrilegious presumption for anyone below fifty or sixty years of age to sit down at the communion table. This feeling is somewhat modified but it is not yet extinct.

I noted too the great power and numbers of elders in the church. They are often uneducated, strictly evangelical, generally fluent in speech, unctuous in prayer, conscious of power, and sometimes, it has to be said, not indifferent to the good things of life. They owe their power over the labouring class to a gift of prayer, preaching and cate-chising, which, owing nothing to the aid of school and college of learning, but being regarded as heaven-sent, is worthy of deeper reverence than pulpit ministrations of ministers who required to be taught to preach and teach.

While many of these folk were genuinely pious and godly men, who showed great zeal in the discharge of their duties, I must say of some I met that an equally favourable estimate could not be given.

In contrast to and, on occasion alongside, strict religious beliefs, some superstitious practices persist, although I am told that they have decreased in recent times.

A girl in a school I visited had the bone of her arm broken by falling over a form in the classroom. After twenty-one days had elapsed the doctor was sent for and found a thread with three knots lying on the fracture, over which, while knotting it an old woman pronounced some Gaelic verses. Many otherwise sensible people wear knotted threads on parts of their body as preventatives or cures of disease. It is possible that the knots have survived from Catholic times of the beads of the rosary.

The doctor was called in to see a woman who had some outbreak on her face. On asking her to uncover her face he found it presented a most ghastly appearance, being all smeared with the blood of a black cock. This unfortunate fowl is a sovereign remedy for many troubles I have learned and it is sometimes, in a vicarious way, buried alive!

To cure dropsy, a bottle of water is brought from a well in an island in Loch Maree, and in the presence of the sufferer broken against a rock that had never been moved. The efficacy of this cure was tested within a few hundred yards of the residence of my informant three days before.

A man had a child suffering from water in the head, and carried him on his back in a blanket over 120 miles to see a man who professed to cure ailments. He was given a bottle of water, a spoonful of which was to be given three times a day. On finding out about it the doctor discovered the water to be absolutely putrid.

Many of the common people would not count their chickens or pro-nounce a baby pretty without first blessing it. The blessing is said to disarm the evil eye. The Irish Celt I have learned has the same super-stition.

To this day there is very strong objection in the Highlands to a funeral procession taking any but the longest usual road to the churchyard. Even where a new modern road has been laid, the former would be used for the funeral, as there is the belief that another inmate of the house would die before the lapse of a year.

I do not know what consequences might be expected from a contre-temps which I heard of recently. A number of men in funeral garb were standing without apparent object, at a railway station. The porter, on being asked for an explanation, said, 'Oh there was to have been a funeral, but the corpse has missed the connection.'

Examination in Singing.   57

DIVISION II.

1. *Note Test.*—To sing slowly, as pointed out by the Examiner, and using the Sol-fa syllables, the ascending and descending notes of the scale of C, the notes of the key-chord of C (*Doh, Mi, Soh, Doh*), in any order, and also small groups of consecutive notes of the scale of C as written by the Examiner.

Examples:—

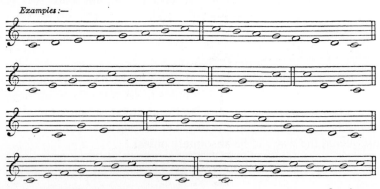

2. *Time Test.*—To sing on one sound, to the syllable *laa* or *doh*, an exercise in $\frac{2}{4}$ or $\frac{4}{4}$ time. which shall include minims and crotchets.

Example:—

3. *Ear Test.*—To repeat (that is, imitate, not name) a simple phrase of not more than four notes, using the syllable *laa*, after hearing the examiner sing (or play) it twice through.

(from the Annotated Scotch Code)

Temperance.

and diseases of the liver, among persons engaged in different occupations, demonstrating the relatively high mortality from alcoholism in certain trades as compared with what may be thought of as the standard mortality for occupied males of all trades and professions.

Occupation.	All Causes.		Alcoholism and Diseases of the Liver.	
	1890–1892.	1900–1902.	1890–1892.	1900–1902.
Occupied males	100	100	100	100
Coachman, cabman . . .	121	115	149	137
Costermonger	173	192	160	222
Coalheaver	160	124	162	117
Fishmonger	101	102	164	173
Musician	127	123	166	195
Dock labourer	192	149	191	168
Chimney sweep	138	134	200	180
Butcher	115	115	219	217
Brewer	150	143	251	280
Inn-servant	181	191	413	424
Inn-keeper	172	180	717	724

Note 2.—The following Table shows the Expectancy of Life (that is, the average future duration of life dated from the age in question)—(*a*) in the general population of England and Wales based on the experience of 1891-1900, (*b*) in persons insured in a large number of the principal Life Offices based on the experience of 1863-93, and (*c*) in various Friendly Societies and the United Kingdom Temperance and General Provident Institution. It will be seen how much more favourable is the Expectancy of Life in persons abstaining from the use of alcoholic beverages :—

Age.	General Expectancy of Total Male Population in England and Wales based on Experience of 1891-1900. (Registrar-General.)	General Expectancy based on the Experience of Persons insured in a large Number of the Principal Life Offices in Great Britain in Years 1863-93. (Institute of Actuaries.)	Odd-fellows. (Non-abstainers largely.)	Foresters. (Non-abstainers largely.)	Recha-bites. (Ab-stainers.)	United Kingdom Temperance and General Provident Institution based on Experience of 1841-1901. (Abstainers.)
20	41·0	43·2	41·4	43·1	48·8	46·9
25	37·0	39·1	37·6	39·0	44·3	43·0
30	33·1	35·1	34·0	34·8	39·7	38·3
35	29·2	31·2	30·3	30·7	35·1	34·6
40	25·6	27·4	26·8	26·7	30·6	30·3
45	22·2	23·7	23·3	22·8	26·1	26·1
50	18·9	20·1	19·9	19·1	21·8	22·0
55	15·8	16·7	16·6	—	17·7	18·1
60	12·9	13·6	13·6	—	13·8	14·6

The first column of this Table gives the expectancy of life of the general population, whether insured or not. For instance, a person out of the general population at the age of 20 may expect to live 41 years more. The second column gives the expectancy of life as experienced by a large number of insured persons chiefly of a social status above the wage-earning classes, and it will be seen that the expectancy of life is somewhat increased at each age. With these may be compared the experience of the two great Friendly Societies (Oddfellows and Foresters), of whom a high proportion are non-abstainers, and the experience of the relatively small society of the Rechabites consisting only of abstainers. The last column gives the experience of abstaining persons chiefly of small means or who are insured for small sums. Comparing the last two columns with the first four columns it will be noted that the abstainers show a much higher expectancy of life than any of the other groups at each age and in all cases.

Further, it has been ascertained by the Registrar-General that of 61,215 men between 25 and 65 in the community, 1,000 die in one year ; but of 61,215 publicans, 1,642 die in one year,

Statistical information provided for teachers when talking about alcohol abuse

No. on Register	Date of Admission or Re-admission.						Name of Child in Full.	Name of Parent or Guardian.	Address of Parent or Guardian
	Day.	Mo.	Year.	Day.	Mo.	Year.			
1	2	12	75				Hugh Mackay	Hector Mackay	Eriboll
2	2	12	75				Evander Mackay	"	"
3	2	12	75				John Murdo Mackay		
4	3	12	75				George Sinclair	Angus Sinclair	Anaboll
5	3	12	75				John Sinclair		
6	3	12	75				William Sinclair		
7	6	12	75				John M'Intosh	John M'Intosh	Cashildhu
8	15	12	75				Angus Sutherland	John Sutherland	Eriboll
9	2	12	75				Christina Mackay	Hector Mackay	
10	3	12	75				Johan Sinclair	Angus Sinclair	Anabol
11	3	12	75				Jane Sinclair		
12	13	12	75				Tomina Mackay	Donald Mackay	Hielam
13	13	12	75				Margaret Mackay		
14	20	12	75				Jessie Mackay		
15	2	3	76				Christopher Mackay	Angus Mackay	Laid
16	2	3	76				Hugh Mackay		
17	6	3	76				James Mackay	George Mackay	Portnacon
18	6	3	76				Roderick Sutherland	George Mackay	Laid
19	7	3	76				John Mackay	Donald Mackay	Carriekdhu
20	7	3	76				Angus McLeod	Donald McLeod	Rhigoller
21	8	3	76				Hugh Stewart	Peter Stewart	Laid
22	9	3	76				Angus Mackay	Charles Mackay	"
23	14	3	76				William Mackay	Donald Mackay	Portnacon
24	2	3	76				Mary Mackay	Angus Mackay	Laid
25	6	3	76				Jane Stewart (a)	Peter Stewart	"
26	6	3	76				Tomina Stewart	Ewen Stewart	
27	6	3	76				Jessie Stewart (a)		
28	6	3	76				Jane Stewart (b)	Donald Stewart	"
29	6	3	76				Jessie Stewart (b)		
30	6	3	76				Margaret Stewart		"
31	6	3	76				Johan Mackay	Donald Campbell	
32	6	3	76				Effie Gunn	John Gunn	
33	13	3	76				Barbara Gunn	Hughina Gunn	Portnacon
34	14	3	76				Christina McDonald	Archibald McDonald	Polla

Extract from the 1875 Register of Admission, Laird Public School, Sutherland

XXII

In Conclusion

A retrospect of the past forty years fills me not unreasonably with a very large measure of content. While it represents a good deal of hard work it also recalls the memory of many congenial friendships, and of much enjoyment which has left no aftertaste of bitterness. It is accompanied by consciousness of having been engaged in important work, of having tried with more or less success to do it, and of having retired from it physically and mentally sound, before the capacity for enjoyment was exhausted. The result of it all is that, were it possible to put back the hands of the clock, I would cheerfully go through it again.

I do not forget that someone has said that a great book (meaning large) is a great evil. It falls to the lot of a few to be the author of a great book. My ambition takes no such lofty flight. It would have been easy to make this one larger, but it is probably large enough for all the really useful matter it contains. I have put down, as they occurred to me, such a selection of my experiences – some perhaps useful, others amusing – as might be fairly readable. If I have succeeded in this, and especially if I have said anything that may be useful to teachers or younger members of the inspectorate, I shall not regret the employment I have made of my leisure.

And now for the present I lay down my pen.